355.

·N·U·C·L·E·A·R·
·W·E·A·P·O·N·S·

Bernard Harbor
and
Chris Smith

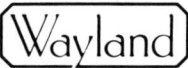

Points of View

Advertising
Alcohol
Animal Rights
Apartheid
Censorship
Divorce
Drugs

Medical Ethics
Northern Ireland
Nuclear Weapons
Racism
Sex and Sexuality
Smoking
Terrorism

Front cover: *A desert-test of a nuclear bomb. The mushroom cloud created by nuclear explosions has come to symbolize the threat posed by nuclear weapons.*

ac. 6367

Editor: William Wharfe
Designer: David Armitage

First published in 1989 by
Wayland (Publishers) Limited
61 Western Road, Hove
East Sussex BN3 1JD, England

© Copyright 1989 Wayland (Publishers) Limited

British Library Cataloguing in Publication Data
Harbor, Bernard
    Nuclear weapons. — (Points of view)
    1. Nuclear weapons
    I. Title II. Smith, Chris, *1955*– III. Series
    355.8'25119

ISBN 1-85210-650-6

Phototypeset by Direct Image Photosetting Ltd,
Hove, East Sussex, England.
Printed in Italy by G. Canale & C.S.p.A., Turin
Bound in France by A.G.M.

Contents

1	Introduction	4
2	The effects of nuclear war	9
3	Keeping the peace ?	16
4	The spread of nuclear weapons	20
5	Nuclear weapons: right or wrong ?	26
6	Arms control and disarmament	30
7	'Star wars'	38
8	Conclusion	42

Glossary	46
Further information	47
Index	48

Introduction

> We knew the world could not be the same. A few people laughed, a few people cried. Most people were silent. I remembered the line from the Hindu scripture, the *Bhagavad Gita*: 'Now I am become death, destroyer of worlds'. (Robert Oppenheimer, US scientist who helped develop the world's first atomic bomb.)

This is how the scientist Robert Oppenheimer described the reaction of his team of scientists when the first nuclear bomb was detonated in 1945 in the desert in New Mexico, USA. A few months later two more nuclear bombs were detonated when they were dropped on the two Japanese cities of Hiroshima and Nagasaki, with devastating consequences for the people of those cities and for the whole world. This was both the end of the Second World War and the beginning of the nuclear age. As Oppenheimer said, the world could not be the same again.

Below *Two months after the first atom bomb test, in 1945, scientists measure radioactivity in the sand (Robert Oppenheimer is third from the left).*

Above *The crew of the* Enola Gay, *the aeroplane that dropped the first atom bomb on Hiroshima, on 6 August, 1945.*

For a brief period after the Second World War the USA was the only country with nuclear weapons. But by 1949 the Soviet Union had also developed its nuclear bomb, and China, Britain and France followed. Today, the military world is still dominated by the two 'superpowers': the USA and the Soviet Union. These two countries possess over 95 per cent of the world's nuclear weapons, which have a combined destructive force equivalent to 65,000 billion tons of conventional TNT explosive.

During the Second World War the USA and the Soviet Union were allies in the fight against fascism. Soon after the war, however, the differences and disagreements between the two countries began to divide them more and more. Without a common enemy it was impossible for the two political and economic systems (of capitalism in the USA and communism in the Soviet Union) to remain friendly. Relations between the two countries worsened throughout the 1940s and 1950s and developed into what became known as the Cold War. The term 'Cold War' described the situation where relations between the two countries were as tense as they could be without a war actually breaking out.

Following the Second World War, Europe and the superpowers were divided into two political camps. NATO (the North Atlantic Treaty Organization) grouped together the USA, Canada and most of the countries of Western Europe. The Soviet Union and most of the countries of Eastern Europe were grouped together by the Warsaw Pact. In other parts of the world many countries became aligned with either the 'East' (the Warsaw Pact) or the 'West' (NATO), though the alignment was not always formalized by treaties or alliances. Countries like Australia, New Zealand and Japan supported, and were supported by, NATO countries. Cuba, Vietnam and others have, over the years, become allies of the Warsaw Pact.

Some countries, mostly but not exclusively outside Europe, have decided not to be too closely associated with either of the political groupings. These non-aligned countries include China, India, Sweden, Switzerland, Yugoslavia, Brazil and many other, less powerful, nations.

Above *In May 1952, 2000 American Marines participated in this nuclear weapons test. They were unwittingly exposed to dangerously high levels of radioactivity.*

Left *After the Second World War, the British, American and Soviet leaders (left to right Atlee, Truman and Stalin) at the Potsdam conference in Germany (July–August 1945) where they decided the post-war settlement of Europe. However, such friendly relations did not last.*

Right *A test launch of the Trident nuclear missile from Cape Canaveral, Florida, USA. Trident is designed to be launched from nuclear submarines.*

As nuclear arsenals have grown in size and sophistication, nuclear weapons have dominated military and political thinking. Few military or political decisions can now be made without reference to nuclear weapons. This is not only in terms of relations between the two superpowers or the two military alliances of NATO and the Warsaw Pact. It also affects relationships between the superpowers and other countries, including developing countries. Issues involving nuclear weapons may alter relationships between countries within alliances; for example, relations between New Zealand and the USA have been soured by New Zealand's policy of not allowing nuclear weapons on its territory.

Political decisions inside countries are also affected by the nuclear situation. The nuclear question and more general military matters affect political and economic choices about many other issues; for example, should scarce resources be spent on weapons or on schools and hospitals? Because of the possibility of nuclear weapons falling into the hands of enemies or terrorists, elaborate security forces and secret services have been built up in both nuclear and non-nuclear nations. As a result, secrecy has become a normal part of government.

Nuclear weapons have affected much more than military, political and economic systems. The effects on all aspects of culture have been wide-ranging. It has been said that the mushroom cloud which is created by a nuclear explosion is 'the most compelling image of our time'. The nuclear issue has intruded into the world of films, books, plays and pop music just as much as into the political world.

The nuclear bomb has had a major effect on the way we, as ordinary people, think about our world, our place in the world and our future. In 1988, a survey conducted in ten countries found that one third of young people lived in fear of nuclear weapons, while one third of adults expected that nuclear war would happen in their lifetime.

In this book we will look in some detail at a wide range of opinions about the various aspects of nuclear weapons. We will be asking: What are nuclear weapons for? Do they keep the peace? What would happen if nuclear war broke out? Is it right for countries to have nuclear weapons? Will they spread around the globe? Finally, what needs to be done in order to rid the world of nuclear weapons?

Left *The horror of Hiroshima as depicted by a Japanese artist.*

2 The effects of nuclear war

The only time nuclear weapons have been used was on Japan during the Second World War. Only two, relatively small, atom bombs were dropped on the two cities. Both were destroyed and over 200,000 people died in Hiroshima alone.

> 'Little Boy', the U235 bomb which annihilated Hiroshima, was small by modern standards: its yield was about 13kt [equivalent to 13,000 tons of TNT]. By contrast, a modern Polaris missile has a yield of 660kt, the cruise missile of 200kt. So it is well to remember that when governments and soldiers describe fighting limited nuclear wars with 'small' bombs, the very least they mean is to repeat Hiroshima. What happened there?

'Little Boy' was dropped at 8.15 am. Immediately, a huge mushroom cloud was seen over the city of Hiroshima. The blast blew many people against buildings, while others, trying to flee, were crushed beneath falling stone. Half an hour later, a fire storm began to blow, and by late morning a tornado had developed. Over an area of some 400 km² a 'black rain' fell.

Left *Hiroshima photographed immediately after being hit by an atom bomb, August, 1945. The bomb was tiny by today's standards.*

Above *Nothing is safe from an atomic blast. Here a survivor in Hiroshima inspects the wreck of a bus, shortly after the explosion.*

The temperature dropped dramatically, so that many people shivered although it was midsummer . . .

The extent of destruction is difficult to imagine, let alone measure . . . It is likely that half of the casualties were caused by burns of one type or another. Most of the people who died in this excruciating way did so after only a few days, deprived of medical care. Others were roasted alive or died of asphyxiation in the firestorm . . .

The survivors, the *hibakusha,* live distorted and broken lives. They have proved more prone to cancers and leukaemia than the rest of the Japanese population, so even those who appeared to have survived the bombings are truly victims. (The Committee for the Compilation of Materials on Damage Caused by the Atomic Bombs on Hiroshima and Nagasaki, 1981.)

Everybody hopes that nuclear weapons will never be used again. But as long as some countries possess them the chance of nuclear war — by intent or accident — cannot be ruled out. So, it is important to appreciate the effects of a nuclear war. The horrific damage caused by nuclear weapons also encourages us to think very carefully about disarmament and arms control.

The effects of nuclear war

Nuclear weapons cause death and destruction in six main ways: a) Burns, b) Firestorms, c) Blast, d) Immediate lethal doses of radiation, e) Long-term radiation fall-out, f) Electro-magnetic pulse.

For many years after the invention of nuclear weapons most people thought of them as huge bombs which, when used, would create tremendous destruction on explosion. This is true but, in addition, a nuclear weapon has more lasting effects, such as fall-out, which may under certain circumstances be more dangerous than the initial blast. Those who wish to limit or do away completely with nuclear weapons have stressed the range of immediate and long-term effects of nuclear weapons. Others have attempted to play down the long-term risks.

In the immediate aftermath of a nuclear war there would be widespread devastation.

> In a 2-megaton explosion over a fairly large city, buildings would be vaporized, people reduced to atoms and shadows, outlying structures blown down like matchsticks and raging fires ignited . . .

Below *Some survivors of Hiroshima demonstrate against nuclear weapons in New York City in 1988. People even now are suffering because of the nuclear attack in 1945.*

Above *American scientist Carl Sagan.*

Below *A 20 kiloton nuclear device detonated (in a test in 1980) 300 m below the surface caused this massive crater — 30 m deep and over 100 m across.*

[In the case of a full scale nuclear war.] The World Health Organization concludes that 1.1 billion people would be killed outright in such a nuclear war, mainly in the United States, the Soviet Union, Europe, China and Japan. An additional 1.1 billion people would suffer serious injuries and radiation sickness, for which medical help would be unavailable. It thus seems possible that more than 2 billion people — almost half of the humans on earth — would be destroyed in the immediate aftermath of a global nuclear war. (Carl Sagan, scientist, author and disarmament campaigner, *The Nuclear Winter.*)

A nuclear war would also mean more than the widespread destruction of people and property. Such a war would have equally serious long-term effects, particularly on the environment. Sophisticated computer modelling conducted recently indicates that in the aftermath of a nuclear war the whole world would be enveloped in a 'nuclear winter'.

> The results of our calculations astonished us. . . . the amount of sunlight on the ground was reduced to a few per cent of normal — much darker, in daylight, than in a heavy overcast and too dark for plants to make a living from photosynthesis.

The effects of nuclear war

Above *When Mount St Helens erupted in 1980 huge quantities of dust were released into the atmosphere, affecting weather around the world. The amount of dust thrown up during a nuclear war could cause catastrophic changes in the weather.*

There are numerous examples of accidents and incidents involving nuclear weapons and nuclear war. For example, in 1960 a radar malfunction involving the US early warning system in Greenland incorrectly warned the US of a massive Soviet missile strike. In 1968 a G-class Soviet ballistic missile submarine exploded and sank in the Black Sea.

At least in the Northern Hemisphere . . . a deadly gloom would persist for months. Even more unexpected were the temperatures calculated. In the baseline case, land temperatures . . . dropped to minus 25° Celcius (minus 13° Farenheit) and stayed below freezing for months — even for a summer war. . . . because the temperatures would drop so catastrophically, at least in the Northern Hemisphere, virtually all crops and farm animals would be destroyed, as would most varieties of uncultivated or undomesticated food supplies. Most of the human survivors would starve. (*The Nuclear Winter.*)

Furthermore, to add to the misery, the radiation released by nuclear explosions would contaminate water and food supplies, which would have the effect of destroying the food chain.

Not everybody believes in the doomsday scenario portrayed by the scientists. The scientific basis of the famous nuclear winter has been criticized and the dispute has become extremely complicated. A less direct form of criticism can be seen amongst those who feel that a nuclear war is survivable, providing effective measures are taken in the form of civil defence. This is also the view of many governments.

Most governments that possess nuclear weapons stress that war will be prevented by deterrence (see chapter three). But they concede that should deterrence fail, measures can be taken to protect lives. Basically, this involves the building of nuclear shelters and, for the less fortunate, protective measures in the home. According to one of former US President Reagan's officials in 1981, people should:

> Dig a hole, cover it with a couple of doors and then throw three feet of dirt on top . . . It's the dirt that does it . . . if there are enough shovels to go around, everybody's going to make it. (T.K. Jones, US Under Secretary of Defense for Strategic and Theater Nuclear Forces, 1981.)

The British government also thinks that protection is possible, but offers advice in a less dramatic fashion:

> Make a 'lean-to' with sloping doors (taken from rooms above) or strong boards, rested against an inner wall. Prevent them from slipping by fixing a length of wood along the floor. Build further protection of bags or boxes of earth or sand — or books or even clothing — on the slope of your refuge, and anchor these also against slipping. Partly close the two open ends with boxes of earth or sand, or heavy furniture. (*Protect and Survive*, British government pamphlet.)

---

1 Can you imagine what would happen to your home town if it became the target for a nuclear strike? What would be the combined effect upon homes, factories, shops, public services and buildings?

2 We all make mistakes. Discuss the possibility of a nuclear war occurring by accident.

3 Do you think that civil defence might make nuclear war more likely if more people feel that they could survive?

A nuclear shelter in the USA. Some Americans do not consider doors, dirt and shovels to be adequate protection against nuclear attack (see quotation above).

The effects of nuclear war

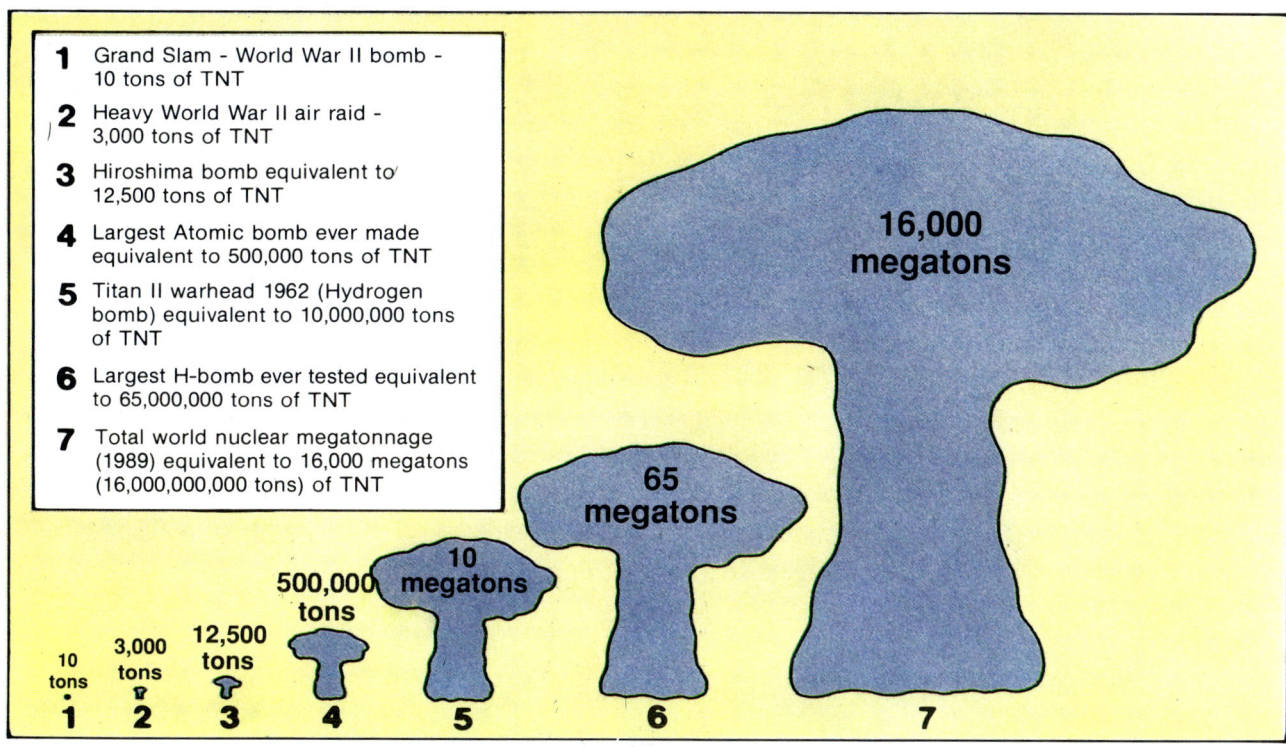

This diagram shows how the destructive power of nuclear weapons has increased since the Second World War.

Possibly, measures such as these might provide a small amount of protection, but it is highly likely that there would be too little time to make adequate preparations; that houses would not withstand the effects of blast; and all radio and television communications would break down. This would leave the survivors with no information on how to proceed after a nuclear attack. Still more important, there would be no medical facilities or doctors, no food or water supplies and no police force to maintain law and order. Civilization as we know it would be destroyed.

> Our fine great buildings, our homes would exist no more. The thousands of years it took to develop our civilization will have been in vain . . . there will be no help, there will be no hope. (Earl Mountbatten, one-time British Chief of Defence Staff.)

Consequently, whenever we think about or discuss nuclear war we should always be aware of the tremendous environmental and human suffering which would be involved in even the smallest of nuclear exchanges — nuclear weapons are powerful enough to destroy the world.

3 Keeping the peace?

Throughout history many scientists and politicians have dreamt of developing a weapon so terrible that it would be unthinkable to go to war. In 1945, when the enormous destructive power of the atom bomb was demonstrated to the world at Hiroshima and Nagasaki, most people believed that the ultimate weapon had now been invented and that wars could no longer be fought.

By the 1950s the two superpowers, the USA and the Soviet Union, both possessed nuclear weapons, and policies of nuclear deterrence emerged. Deterrence meant that no country would use nuclear weapons against another, because if it did, the country which it attacked would respond with nuclear weapons. The use of nuclear weapons on another country would, therefore, guarantee a nuclear attack on one's own, resulting in unacceptable death and destruction. As no country could hope to survive a nuclear war, no country would start one.

> Countries with advanced nuclear weapon programmes which are or may be seeking nuclear weapons: Argentina, Brazil, India, Pakistan and South Africa.
>
> Examples of countries with fewer capabilities but with an interest in nuclear weapons: Iran, Iraq, Libya.

This map shows the size of the NATO and Warsaw Pact nuclear armouries.

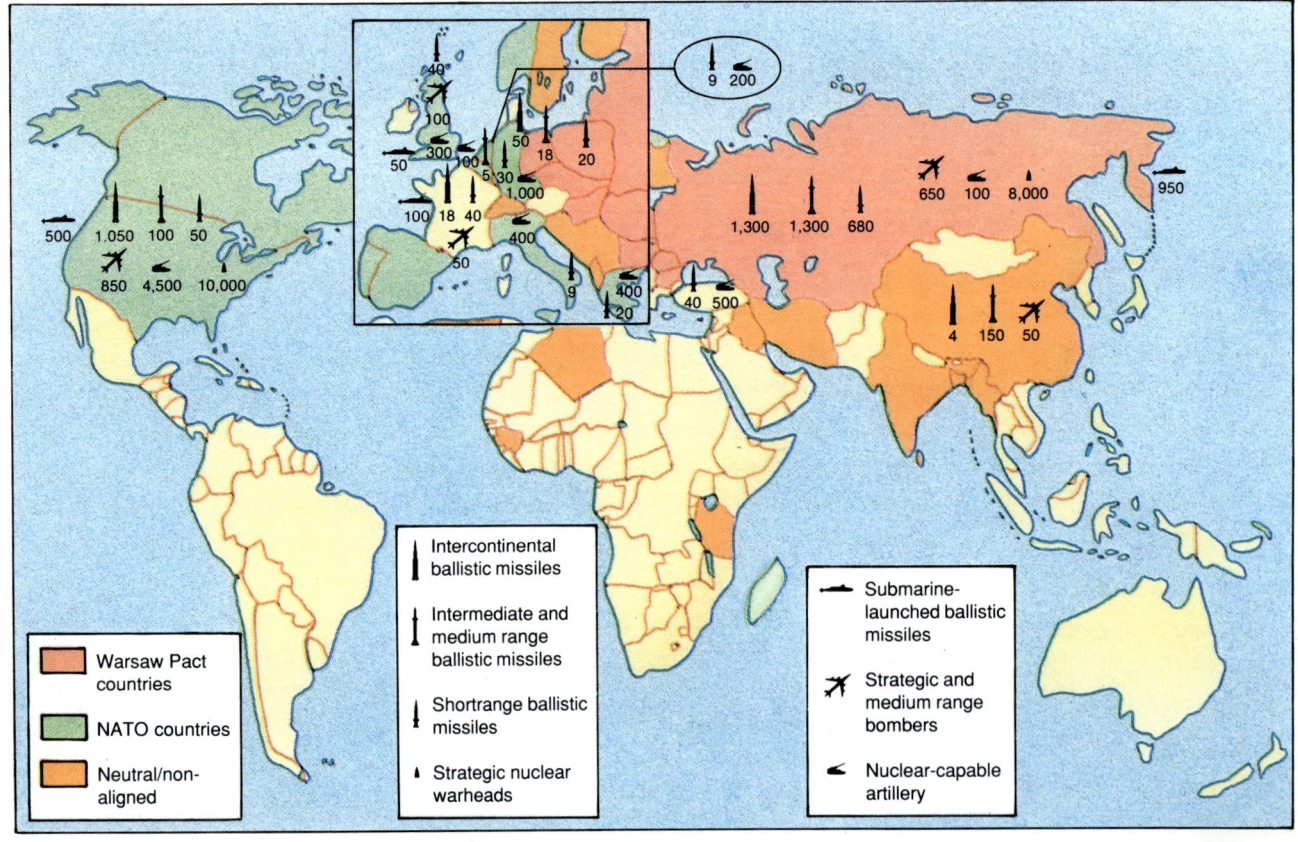

Keeping the peace?

One of the first NATO military exercises. American tanks on the move in West Germany, November 1950.

There are many different types of nuclear weapon but they can be broadly divided into three types:

1 Strategic nuclear weapons which would be used in an all-out nuclear war. They include ballistic missiles that can be launched from the ground or from submarines (and which leave the earth's atmosphere before coming back down and hitting their targets); and bombs dropped from aeroplanes.

2 Intermediate nuclear weapons which are based on the ground, on submarines or on aeroplanes, but which have a much shorter range than strategic missiles. These do not leave the earth's atmosphere before hitting their targets.

3 Battlefield nuclear weapons. These are the smallest type and are designed to be used in the battlefield. Often they are fired by equipment which can also fire non-nuclear weapons.

Since the end of the Second World War no wars have been fought in Europe and this is seen by many people as proof that nuclear weapons have kept the peace. One British prime minister has said:

> There are fears about the terrible destructive power of nuclear weapons. But it is the balance of nuclear forces that has preserved peace for forty years in a Europe which twice in the previous thirty years tore itself to pieces; the nuclear balance which has preserved peace not only from nuclear war but from conventional war in Europe as well. (Prime Minister Margaret Thatcher, October 1986.)

As stocks of nuclear weapons have grown and political differences have remained, however, many people believe that this idea of deterrence is far too simple and that, although no war has been fought in Europe in this period, nuclear weapons do not guarantee that this will always be the case. Rather, the existence of these weapons may eventually result in nuclear conflict.

> An arms race reduces the chances that political conflicts can be resolved peacefully . . . The deployment of more capable weapons can persuade an adversary not only that it confronts enhanced military capabilities, but also that there is an increased likelihood that its enemy intends to make use of those capabilities. Then the observing state may decide that it must acquire similar or greater military capabilities. The resulting arms competition increases political tension. In extreme circumstances, one of the nations may conclude that war is inevitable, that the balance of military power is likely to worsen in the future, and that it should take pre-emptive military action to remove the threat poised against it. *(Common Security: A Programme for Disarmament,* produced by the Independent Commission on Disarmament and Security Issues, chaired by Olof Palme, 1982.)

Furthermore, as nuclear strategy has developed over the last forty years, policies have developed which suggest that a limited use of nuclear weapons would be possible in certain circumstances:

> It would be our policy to use nuclear weapons wherever we felt it necessary to protect our forces and achieve our objectives. (Robert McNamara, US Secretary for Defense, 1962.)

There were three nuclear weapons made in 1945, today there are over 60,000 in the world.

The nuclear bomb which was dropped on Hiroshima killed some 80,000 people instantly and injured over 100,000 more. The entire city was destroyed and the long-lasting effects of radiation poisoning killed many more people in the years after the attack. Today, the world's nuclear arsenal contains the equivalent of more than one million Hiroshima bombs.

Since 1945 over 20 million people have been killed in conventional wars throughout the world.

The modern nuclear deterrent: a submarine carrying Trident missiles, with its missile tubes open.

American troops in action during the Vietnam War (1950–75), which claimed 1.3 million Vietnamese and 56,000 American lives. Although there has been peace in Europe since the Second World War, major wars have been fought in other parts of the world.

> The United States has never ruled out a first use of nuclear weapons. If an enemy, whether by stealth and deception or by large-scale mobilization, should attempt to defeat US and allied conventional forces, it is NATO and US policy to take whatever action is necessary to restore the situation. (Donald Rumsfeld, US Secretary for Defense, 1977.)

This idea is very different from the original concept of deterrence and has been strongly challenged:

> There is no illusion more dangerous than the idea that nuclear war can still serve as an instrument of policy, that one can attain political aims by using nuclear weapons and at the same time get off scot-free oneself or that acceptable forms of nuclear war can be found. (Soviet Major General Talenski, May 1965.)

The policy of nuclear deterrence depends on each country making assessments of both the capabilities and intentions of its adversaries. There is always the possibility that politicians and soldiers may make errors of judgement or that there may be technical failures in military equipment. Added to these inherent uncertainties are the complicated military plans of countries which consider the use of some nuclear weapons in some circumstances. If it is indeed nuclear weapons which have kept the peace in Europe, that peace seems very unstable.

Furthermore, the possession of nuclear weapons has not prevented countries from going to war in other parts of the world. Since the Second World War the USA has fought in Vietnam; the Soviet Union in Afghanistan; the Chinese in India; the French in North Africa; and Britain in the Falklands. Nuclear weapons could not prevent these wars; neither could they be used in them.

1 When the Swedish engineer Nobel invented the explosive dynamite he believed that it was a weapon so terrible that wars could no longer be fought. Do you think nuclear weapons may succeed in preventing major wars, because they are so destructive?

2 What factors, other than nuclear weapons, might have helped prevent war in Europe since 1945?

3 Do you think that the limited use of nuclear weapons would be possible in a war or would it naturally lead to an all-out nuclear war?

4 The spread of nuclear weapons

For the first twenty years after the Second World War all the countries with nuclear weapons were members of NATO and the Warsaw Pact. However, over time, other countries became technologically and industrially more advanced and realized that they could manufacture nuclear weapons. In 1964 China conducted its first nuclear test and soon developed its own nuclear weapons. In the 1970s several other countries, such as Israel and Pakistan, were judged to be producing at least the capability to develop nuclear weapons if not the actual weapons themselves.

Many people see nuclear proliferation (more nuclear weapons distributed amongst more countries) as a growing threat to world peace. For those countries facing hostile nations that are on the verge of going nuclear, the spread of nuclear weapons is a major political issue.

This map shows how many countries possess or could produce nuclear weapons.

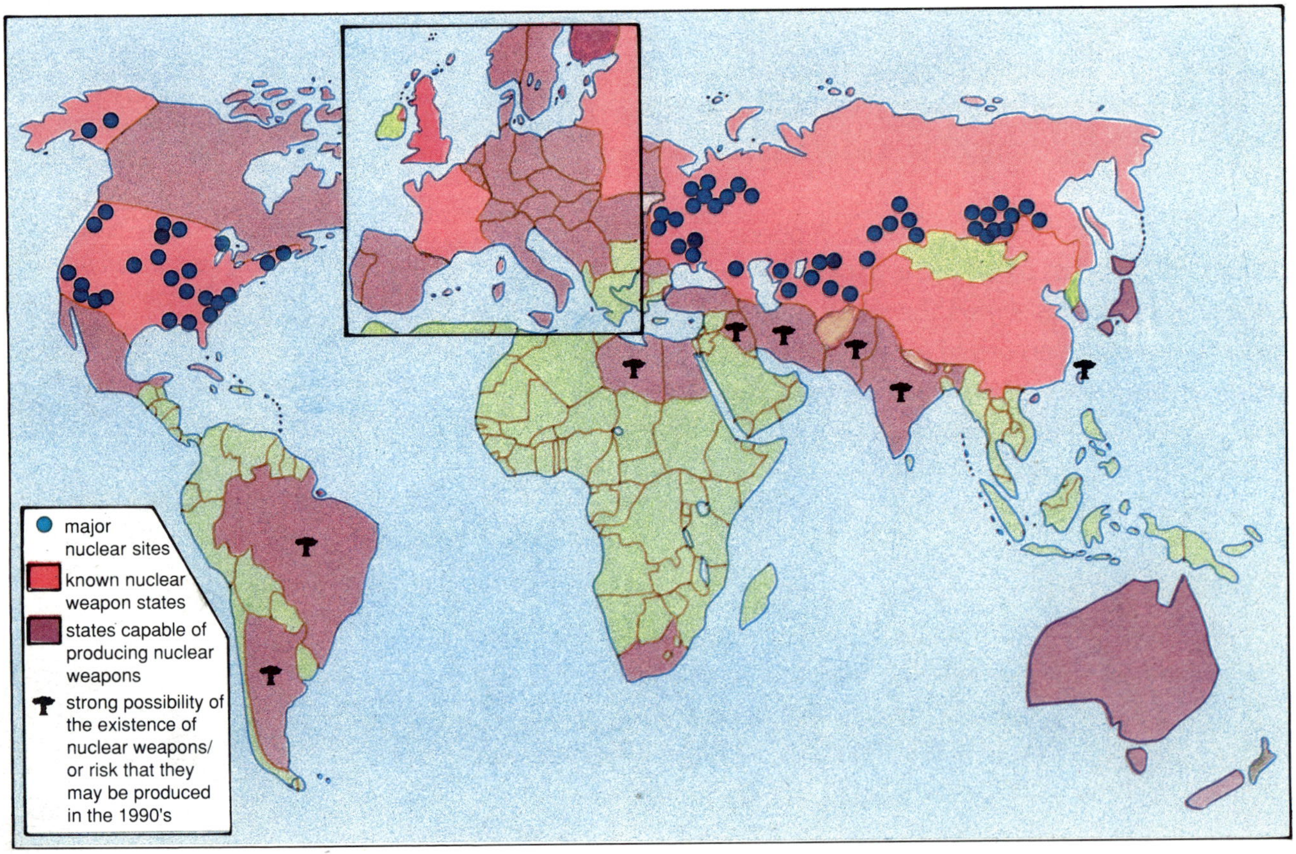

- major nuclear sites
- known nuclear weapon states
- states capable of producing nuclear weapons
- strong possibility of the existence of nuclear weapons/ or risk that they may be produced in the 1990's

The spread of nuclear weapons

According to the just war theory a war is only justified if:
a) It is declared by those with the authority and the knowledge to make a proper judgement.
b) All available peaceful means of settling the dispute have been tried and have failed.
c) It is fought for the sake of a just cause.
d) The harm which will result from the war will not outweigh the good.

> Before the end of this century, a score of nations could possess nuclear weapons. If this should happen, the world we leave our children will mock our own hopes for peace. The level of nuclear armaments could grow by tens of thousands, and the same situation could well occur with advanced nuclear weapons. The temptation to use these weapons, for fear that someone else might do first, would be almost irresistible. (Jimmy Carter, US President 1976-1980, Address to the United Nations (UN) General Assembly, 4 October 1977.)

However, many governments in countries that do not have nuclear weapons feel that their security would be increased if they did. They argue that those countries that already have nuclear weapons do not have the right to make judgements about the efforts of others to acquire them. In addition, some countries have attempted to convince the rest of the world that their nuclear programmes are strictly peaceful, not military, and often these arguments are used together to deflect international criticism.

American President Carter (right) and Soviet Leader Brezhnev during the Salt II talks in June 1979.

Once the ability to make an atom bomb has been acquired, there are many ways to 'deliver' it to the target. The atomic explosion seen here is caused by a shell fired from the gun on the right.

During the 1950s when the level of energy required by the world's industries, motor cars, homes and offices increased dramatically, the use of nuclear power was seen as a means of meeting extra demand in a clean, efficient and cost-effective way. At first most of the advanced industrial countries were content to transfer nuclear technology to developing countries such as Iraq and India. It was generally assumed that these countries had neither the expertise nor the desire to develop nuclear weapons. But many countries are now attempting to build nuclear weapons with the technology they have received for nuclear energy.

> As part of the programme of study of nuclear explosions, the Government of India has undertaken to keep itself abreast of developments in this technology, particularly with reference to its use in the fields of mining and earth moving operations. (Statement by the Atomic Energy Commission of India following India's 1974 nuclear test.)

In fact, India's nuclear test in 1974 was intended for military purposes and prompted India's main enemy, Pakistan, to reply by developing its own nuclear weapon programme.

In 1987, world military expenditure reached US$930 billion, or nearly $2 million each minute. Since 1960 the world has spent over US$15 trillion on the arms race.

The spread of nuclear weapons

On the one hand, Pakistan has consistently denied that it is attempting to build a nuclear weapon. On the other, Pakistan's leaders sometimes use the arguments of the American and British national leaders to justify their right to develop nuclear weapons:
> We have learned to purify plutonium. Now we should, with the help of God, produce an explosion. It will stop all danger of war in this region just as the nuclear strength of the two superpowers has eliminated the danger of war betwen them since World War II. (Prime Minister Mohammed Khan Junejo, November 1985.)

Naturally, Western and Soviet leaders do not share this view. For them, proliferation poses three major problems. First, the possession of nuclear weapons increases a country's military strength and thereby makes it less dependent upon the major powers. Second, nuclear strategy becomes more complicated and confused when it is known that more national leaders can order a nuclear attack. (How could the countries under attack be certain in a short space of time which country has mounted the attack?) Third, several of the countries which are close to acquiring nuclear weapons are extremely unstable, and the use of nuclear weapons is considered more likely in regions such as the Middle East and Southern Africa than among the superpowers.

The combined military budgets of the USA and Soviet Union are larger than the entire income of the African continent.

For the cost of one US nuclear weapons test 40,000 community health workers could be trained in developing countries.

The money spent on research for the US star wars programme in 1988 could have provided an elementary school education for 1,400,000 children in Latin America.

Ayatollah Khomeini, who became leader of Iran in 1979. Iran is suspected by some countries to be attempting to produce nuclear weapons.

23

Above *Archbishop Desmond Tutu.*

Below *Britain signed the Non-Proliferation Treaty in 1970. The American and Soviet ambassadors look on.*

> I myself actually fear that in the end, because they [South Africa's whites] are so irrational, they seem to have a Samson complex . . . They are going to pull down the pillars and everybody must go with them . . . If, as most of us believe, they do have a nuclear capability, I don't put it past them to have their own version of a scorched earth policy. (Desmond Tutu, Archbishop of Cape Town, South Africa, January 1986.)

Since 1968 there has been a treaty in operation intended to prevent the spread of nuclear weapons – the Non-Proliferation Treaty. However, the treaty has not worked well so far for three reasons. First, there are simply too many loopholes in the treaty, such as the clause which allows members to leave the treaty at short notice if their security is threatened sufficiently. Second, non-nuclear countries have seen the potential in nuclear weapons and do not want to sign it away:

> A pro-nuclear attitude has taken a strong hold in the Third World not because the devastation of a nuclear war is underestimated, but precisely because it is understood very well. (Prince Sadruddin Aga Khan, former UN High Commissioner for Refugees, 13 April 1985.)

Inside a Cruise missile base in Europe. Many non-nuclear countries have criticized the superpowers for continually modernizing their nuclear armouries, with weapons like Cruise, while expecting other countries to do without them.

> If it was up to me to decide, I would make an atomic bomb and detonate it in front of international observers to demonstrate the extent of technical know-how . . . One hates to see the big powers developing atomic bombs . . . without being able to do the same ourselves. (Former Brazilian Navy Minister Maximiano Fonseca, September 1986.)

Third, in return for not building nuclear weapons, countries expect the existing nuclear weapon states to disarm. Although there has been some progress in this direction recently (see chapter six), many feel that France, Britain, China and the two superpowers have not kept their side of the bargain.

> . . . the Treaty is not a one-way street. In signing it, the nuclear-weapon states parties agreed to pursue in good faith negotiations on effective measures relating to cessation of the nuclear arms race at an early date and to nuclear disarmament. In this respect the implementation of the Treaty has been largely one-sided, to the understandable concern and dissatisfaction of the non-nuclear weapon parties. There must be recognition of the fact that restraint on one side cannot reasonably be demanded in the face of unlimited expansion on the other. (Message from Mr Javier Pérez de Cuellar, Secretary-General of the United Nations, to the Third Review Conference of the Parties to the Treaty on the Non-Proliferation of Nuclear Weapons, September 1985.)

In all likelihood, nuclear proliferation will occur over the next few years, possibly in southern Asia where both India and Pakistan are threatening to move forward their nuclear weapon programmes. At the same time it seems as though the means to control the spread of nuclear weapons (such as the Non-Proliferation Treaty) are not becoming any stronger. This is another disturbing development in the field of nuclear weapons.

1 Is it fair to assume that a country such as Pakistan should be trusted less than France to possess nuclear weapons?

2 Do you think that all countries should join the Non-Proliferation Treaty? Do those that refuse have a good case or should they put the interests of world peace before their own national interest?

5 Nuclear weapons: right or wrong?

Warfare has always caused moral dilemmas. Some say that it is right to fight for the protection of one's family, country or way of life when they come under threat. Others feel the use of force is immoral in any circumstances. Often, those who want to avoid violence accept that in some circumstances it is immoral *not* to fight against particularly evil and ruthless forces. In the American Civil War for example, people such as Quakers, who normally reject the use of violence, were prepared to fight in the war because they saw slavery (opposed by the North and supported by the South) as a greater evil than the war. Similarly, in the Second World War, many people who were against war felt that the evils and ruthlessness of Nazism compelled them to fight.

Above The British 'Committee of 100' encouraged people to withhold taxes that were earmarked for military spending. This badge advertises the 'No taxes for war' campaign.

Left The caption to this 1960 cartoon read, 'Don't you see, they had to find out if it worked . . .'

Nuclear weapons: right or wrong?

In the nuclear age, even the possession of nuclear weapons has raised moral questions:

> We must say without reservation that nuclear weapons are ultimately unacceptable as agents of national security. We can conceive of no circumstances under which the use of nuclear weapons could be justified and consistent with the will of God, and we must therefore conclude that nuclear weapons must also be rejected as means of threat or deterrence. (Statement of Canadian Church Leaders, 14 December 1982.)

On the other hand, it has been argued by some Christians that even the use of nuclear weapons would not necessarily be immoral.

> My view is that the effectiveness of deterrence depends on the option of using nuclear weapons. I argue from the principle of the just war that not every nuclear attack would be an attack on non-combatants: there would be attacks on military targets in which damage could be less than alternative evils when you weigh the consequences.
>
> I readily admit that most uses of nuclear weapons would be immoral, but there are certain uses which would not automatically be ruled out by the just war tradition. (Richard Harris, Bishop of Oxford in the *Guardian*, 7 January 1987.)

Below *Philosopher and veteran peace campaigner Bertrand Russell (left) taking part in a CND demonstration in 1962.*

A 'die in' in New York City, USA. Protests such as these draw people's attention to the effects of nuclear war in order to persuade people that nuclear weapons are immoral.

Others have argued that the possession of nuclear weapons is ethical, as it is the lesser of the evils we face in the nuclear age.

> The ethical position of deterrence is by no means weak. Its baseline is that we live in a dangerous and difficult world. The exigencies of short-term survival are best served by understanding the realities of those conditions that we cannot change quickly. In ethical terms, it can be argued that it is just as sound to accept, and try to deal with realities that we do not know how to change safely, as it is to pronounce such realities unacceptable and in need of fundamental reform. The realities of a knowledge base in which science graduates can draw up workable designs for atomic bombs, and an international anarchy in which war is a constant danger, require immediate responses that do not allow the luxury of awaiting long-term reform. (Barry Buzan, *An Introduction to Strategic Studies*, 1987.)

> We threaten evil in order not to do it, and the doing of it would be so terrible that the threat seems in comparison to be morally defensible. (Michael Walzer, *Just and Unjust Wars*, 1977.)

Nuclear weapons: right or wrong?

It is not only the possession of nuclear weapons or the threat of their use that has raised moral issues about the bomb. The morality of spending vast amounts on nuclear and other weapons has also been a matter for debate, with many people in developing countries dying of starvation every year.

> In its economic effects the arms race is also life-threatening. Demands on the public purse are its most visible sign. There it is in direct competition with the urgent requirements of a growing population for such basic needs as an adequate diet, health support, environmental protection, the education and training that are central to the development process. (Ruth Sivard, US disarmament analyst, 1987.)

Others, while recognizing the cost of nuclear arsenals, see a moral responsibility to keep them.

> Yes of course we of all people passionately support world disarmament, to put an end to that frightful curse which drains the economies of the world by investing its depleting wealth in weapons of destruction on a scale sufficient to blow up every human being on earth twenty times over . . . But no one knows better than the Jewish people about the immorality, not to mention the futility, of unilateral disarmament and its consequences. It was this imbalance in Europe which eventually led to the Holocaust, and to the 20 million victims of history's most devastating war. To leave *yourself* defenceless and *your* life at risk is just as offensive to Jewish moral teachings as to threaten any other innocent human life. And to rely on the protection of others without contributing equally to *their* protection offends against the Golden Rule 'Love your neighbour as yourself' by placing burdens on *him* you are not prepared to bear yourself. (Chief Rabbi Immanuel Jakobovits, 21 November 1982.)

Like the arguments about the military value of deterrence, the debate is difficult because of the complex nature of nuclear planning. From a very simple moral perspective it is easy to reject nuclear weapons. But in this complex world this can simply mean passing the dilemma on to others who have the responsibility for making sure that a country is properly defended against attack. However, it often seems that those who have these responsibilities, and who control the world of nuclear weapons are reluctant to address the more basic moral questions.

Chief Rabbi Immanuel Jakobovits.

1 Is the moral responsibility to prevent war more important than the responsibility to preserve a country's way of life?

2 Is there a moral difference between possessing nuclear weapons and using them?

3 Most of the countries that devote a lot of resources to nuclear weapons do not have the same economic and social problems as the world's poorer countries. The USA does not experience famine and nearly everyone in the Soviet Union can read and write. Should these countries spend less on nuclear weapons and spend more to help the world's poor?

6 Arms control and disarmament

The dangers, costs and proliferation of nuclear weapons since the Second World War have raised great concern about whether or not the possibility exists for nuclear disarmament. Few people are against nuclear disarmament, because the removal and destruction of all nuclear weapons would make the world a safer place. Yet, so far, such a simple goal has proved impossible to achieve. Instead, governments have concentrated on controlling and limiting nuclear weapons rather than on abolishing them altogether. This process is known as arms control or arms limitation.

Basically, there are two approaches to arms control and disarmament. The first is multilateral arms control, which requires the complete agreement amongst all the governments of the countries concerned before weapons are reduced or eliminated. The second is unilateral disarmament, in which a government recognizes that the possession of nuclear weapons cannot be justified, and acts alone in the hope that its example will be followed by others.

Above *The Conference of the British Labour Party. In 1981 the Labour Party Conference voted for a policy of unilateral nuclear disarmament.*

Arms control and disarmament

Eliminating the threat from nuclear weapons is usually considered to be the most important task of both arms control and disarmament. However, attempts have also been made to limit conventional weapons. The most successful attempt so far was the Biological Weapons Convention of 1972, which prohibited the production of biological weapons. It is possibly the only real example of complete disarmament during the nuclear age. In the near future it is hoped that a similar agreement can be reached on chemical weapons. There is now a growing move towards controlling conventional weapons at the East-West level, for three reasons. First, it is becoming clear that success in this area will greatly improve relations between NATO and the Warsaw Pact. Second, the rising cost of non-nuclear weapons is such that many countries are finding it difficult to pay for them and, consequently, are interested in control. Third, any progress on this front will create even more confidence than exists at present and may pave the way for more substantial moves towards conventional and nuclear disarmament. In particular, it will strengthen arguments in favour of nuclear arms control, because many nuclear weapons are deployed to destroy conventional weapons.

Below *Protesters draw public attention to the Iranian chemical weapons casualties arriving for treatment at Heathrow airport in Britain in 1984. Iraq used chemical weapons against Iran during the Iran–Iraq war (1980–88). It is hoped that an international treaty banning chemical weapons will be signed in the early 1990s.*

Above *Relations between the superpowers improved during the late 1980s. Here Soviet Leader Mikhail Gorbachev is seen with American President Ronald Reagan and Vice President George Bush in New York City, USA, 1988.*

Below *Americans protest against the deployment of Trident missiles.*

Multilateral arms control falls into three categories. The first is called bilateral arms control because only two countries are involved, usually the two superpowers. The most well known examples are the first Strategic Arms Limitation Talks (SALT I) signed in 1972 and the INF Treaty to limit the number of intermediate range nuclear weapons in Europe, signed in 1987. The second usually involves the superpowers as they are the most important and powerful nuclear weapon states, but includes their allies and other nuclear weapon states. For example, the Partial Test Ban Treaty signed in 1963 involved Britain as well as the superpowers. The third category involves all states, for instance, the Non-Proliferation Treaty (even though some chose not to sign the treaty). In many instances the United Nations may become involved, as one of its main tasks is to bring about general and complete disarmament.

However, because the superpowers possess most of the world's nuclear weapons, it is bilateral arms control which attracts the most attention, both critical and supportive. It has been argued by some that the superpowers actually use arms control as a means of managing the nuclear arms race.

Arms control and disarmament

The controlled destruction of a Pershing II nuclear missile in accordance with the 1987 INF Treaty. The fuel of the missile is being burned up.

In SALT I, for example, the superpowers reached agreement on the numbers of long range missiles each side could hold. But the upper limits were greater than either side really wanted. Furthermore, completely absent from the talks was any agreement on the number of warheads each missile could contain. As this was the area in which most progress was occurring at the time it meant that the 'successful' arms control agreement did little to slow down the nuclear arms race.

> By no stretch of the imagination can this be called arms limitation. Instead it is a mutually agreed continuation of the arms race, regulated and institutionalized. The competition for quality of nuclear weapons remains totally unregulated, leaving open the avenue for gaming without end. (Alva Myrdal, ex-Swedish Ambassador for Disarmament, *The Game of Disarmament: How the United States and Russia Run the Nuclear Arms Race*, 1976.)

Against this, government officials and politicians responsible for disarmament policy place great faith in a multilateral approach as the only real way to achieve progress.

Eduard Shevadnadze, Soviet Foreign Minister, played a crucial part alongside George Schultz, American Foreign Secretary, in drafting the INF agreement.

> I suggest to you that the best hope for the future is through SALT — a negotiated arms limitation agreement and a subsequent mutual reduction of forces. To me, the alternatives to a SALT agreement are unacceptable: appeasement, economic exhaustion resulting from an arms race, or a nuclear holocaust. (General Richard Ellis, US Army, July 1978, Center for Defense Information, Washington DC.)

> The British Government firmly believe that disarmament is likely to succeed only when it is balanced between countries or groups of countries, when it is verifiable — so that all parties can be sure that there is no cheating — and when it maintains or enhances the security of all. Progress will not be hastened by one-sided gestures. If we abandon or fail to maintain the forces we need to provide for effective deterrence, not only do we jeopardize our security, but we also remove the incentive for the other side to agree to balanced and verifiable reductions. (UK Foreign and Commonwealth Office, *The UK Role in Arms Control: a short guide to British Government policy,* April 1988.)

Arms control and disarmament

Many other countries such as Canada, New Zealand and Australia also agree with multilateral approaches to arms control. But there can be differences. For example, New Zealand refuses to allow nuclear weapons on its territory and has none of its own.

> One of the keys to our thinking in New Zealand is that the nuclear weapons of so-called allies are as dangerous as those of so-called enemies. (Helen Clark, New Zealand MP, 1987 quoted in Ruth Sivard, *World Military and Social Expenditures*, 1987.)

Despite the few successes of multilateral disarmament talks, such as the INF Treaty in 1987, many people are concerned that progress towards arms control and disarmament has been too slow. There have been many failures, such as the Mutual Balanced Force Reductions talks which took fifteen years to decide upon what to negotiate and even so failed to agree upon a treaty! The alternative, some argue, is for individual governments to take the plunge and eliminate their nuclear weapons as a unilateral gesture in the hope that others will follow.

The NATO council in session. NATO is involved in on-going arms control negotiations with the Warsaw Pact.

> The arms race does not proceed by multilateral agreement. Its dynamic springs from unilateral acts of rearmament by individual states or groups of states. By the same token it is reasonable to suppose that the dynamic of disarmament will be provided by unilateral initiatives in the other direction. But it is not a simple question of choosing between a 'multilateralist' or a 'unilateralist' approach, as if they were two mutually exclusive policies. (Alan Litherman, *A Short Guide to Disarmament*, 1982.)

On 7 December, 1988, Mikhail Gorbachev made such a unilateral gesture, announcing substantial cuts in the Warsaw Pact's conventional forces in Eastern Europe. The act caught the West by surprise, and there were a variety of reactions to it.

> . . . the very mention of sweeping troops, artillery, and armor cuts will stir neutralist tendencies in Europe, pull at the ties that bind NATO and incline many Americans to conclude it's safe to pull out of Europe and cut the American defence budget. (Editorial, *Washington Post*, 8 December 1988.)

Below *Soviet Leader Mikhail Gorbachev takes the world by surprise with an announcement of unilateral conventional disarmament of some Warsaw Pact forces in Eastern Europe (at the United Nations in New York in 1988).*

Arms control and disarmament

The destruction of Soviet SS-12 missiles under the INF Treaty.

> What Gorbachev has done by offering to cut conventional forces in Europe unilaterally is to break through the fantasy of the war game. He has played a series of moves which, with a little bit of help from public opinion in the West, may undermine the basic rules. (Mary Kaldor, *New Statesman*, 16 December, 1988.)

Yet, at the same time, it should be noted that Mr Gorbachev has never suggested a unilateral disarmament of Soviet *nuclear* forces.

Most, if not all of the peace movements that have emerged throughout the world over the past ten years believe in unilateral disarmament. Yet, even if the climate for arms control now seems better, it will take a tremendous effort by all countries for nuclear weapons to be eliminated, whichever approach is used.

1 Do you think that it is important for a country to have nuclear weapons as a safeguard against invasion by conventional forces?

2 Do you think that countries should disarm? If so, should they do so multilaterally or unilaterally?

7 'Star wars'

The lack of success in disarmament negotiations and the failure of nuclear nations to take unilateral steps towards disarmament, have led many people to think that it is impossible to rid the world of nuclear weapons. Some have suggested, therefore, that some technical solution to the nuclear dilemma, a way of protecting ourselves from nuclear attack, should be sought. The most famous of these is the Strategic Defence Initiative (SDI), or 'star wars', in the USA. In the speech that started the USA's SDI programme the American president said:

> What if free people could live secure in the knowledge that their security did not rest upon the threat of instant US retaliation to deter a Soviet attack; that we could intercept and destroy strategic ballistic missiles before they reached our own soil or that of our allies?
>
> I call upon the scientific community who gave us nuclear weapons to turn their great talents to the cause of mankind and world peace: to give us the means of rendering these nuclear weapons impotent and obsolete. (Ronald Reagan, US President 1981-1988, 1983.)

If a strategic ballistic missile were fired it would leave the earth's atmosphere and travel through space. It would then re-enter the earth's atmosphere and travel towards its target.

A 'star wars' system would have to identify strategic ballistic missiles and destroy them in space, before they re-entered the earth's atmosphere.

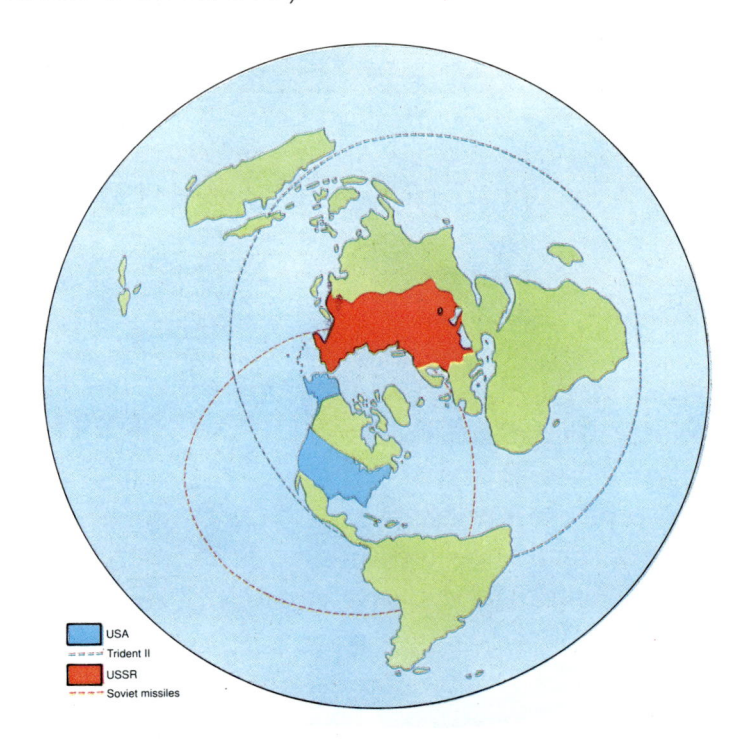

Left *This map shows the ranges of American and Soviet strategic nuclear weapons. With little room for improving their ability to attack one another, one option for the superpowers is to develop defensive systems such as 'star wars'.*

'Star wars'

The idea is that SDI would provide a space-based system to shoot down any nuclear weapons before they could hit their targets. The technology for a system that could guarantee complete defence against nuclear weapons would have to be extremely sophisticated. Because just a tiny malfunction might be catastrophic, many scientists and engineers have expressed doubts that such a system could be built — even if vast amounts of money were spent on it.

> 1. Even a very small percentage of nuclear weapons penetrating a defensive system would cause human suffering and death far beyond that ever before seen on this planet.
> 2. It is likely to be decades, if ever, before an effective, reliable, and survivable defensive system could be deployed.
> 3. Development of prototypes or development of SDI components in a state of technological uncertainty risks enormous waste of financial and human resources.
> (American Physical Society Study Group, 1987.)

This diagram shows how a 'star wars' defence might work. But how would you check that such a system actually works?

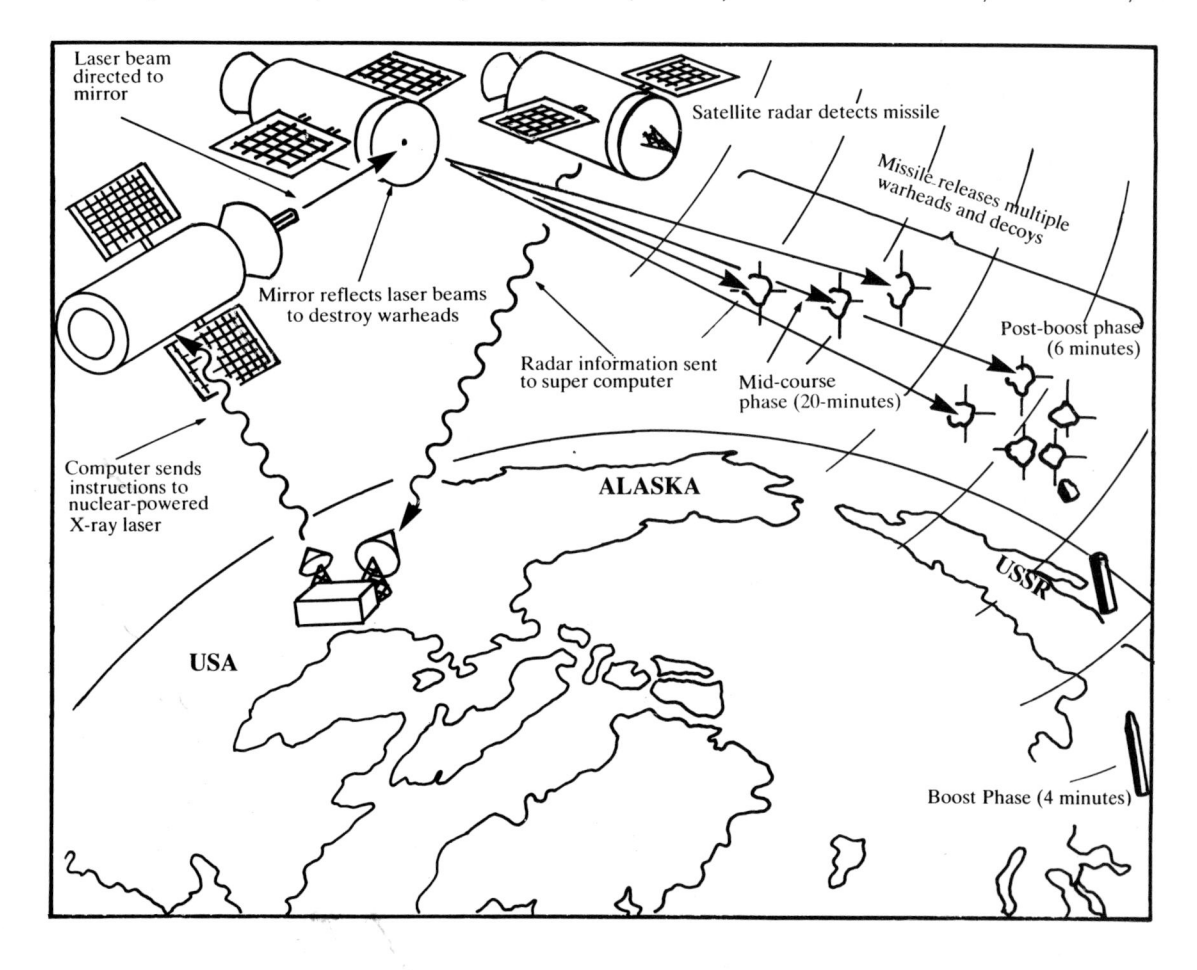

If a 'star wars' system were ever to be put into place it would be the most expensive military system ever built. Because the idea and technology is so new it is impossible to know exactly how much it might cost. However, it has been estimated at between US$400 billion and US$1 trillion.

Californians express their opposition to 'star wars'. The project has run into a lot of opposition in the USA itself.

The 'star wars' idea has also been opposed by those who believe that it would upset the delicate nuclear balance by giving the country with the SDI system an advantage. These people argue that such a system might be seen as defensive to a country that possesses it, but that a country without such protection would be more insecure. Not only would it not have a defensive system, it would not, for a time, be able to prevent a nuclear attack on itself by threatening retaliation. This fear has been so great that in 1972 the superpowers signed a treaty called the Anti-Ballistic Missile (ABM) Treaty which limited the use of such missile defenses. Critics of 'star wars' see the programme as a threat to this treaty and to future progress on disarmament. From a Soviet perspective:

> By implementing the 'star wars' programme, Washington essentially and deliberately aims at wrecking current negotiations and at nullifying all existing agreements on arms reduction. If this happens the USSR and the United States, their allies and the entire world will find themselves, in the coming years, in an absolutely uncontrolled arms race, strategic chaos, undermined stability, and general uncertainty and fear. And, connected with all this, an increased risk of catastrophe. (Soviet Leader Mikhail Gorbachev, 1985.)

1 Imagine that you are the leader of a country with nuclear weapons. Your opponent has a 'star wars' system but you do not. Would you consider your country to be safe from nuclear attack?

2 If a country had a 'star wars' system would it be less likely to work towards disarmament?

3 Which do you think is preferable: a) that all countries have SDI systems; or b) that no country has nuclear weapons?

Right *The space shuttle has been used as an example on both sides of the 'star wars' debate. It has shown what can be achieved through applying sophisticated technology and (with the explosion of the Challenger in 1986) what the consequences are when such equipment goes wrong.*

Casper Weinberger, former American Defense Secretary.

Not surprisingly, US government officials disagree with this negative view of 'star wars':

> I'm not one of those who feels that an active and effective ballistic-missile defense system is destabilizing. The sooner that we can get to it, the better I like it. Obviously if we are able to destroy incoming missiles effectively I don't think it's destabilizing. I think it would be extremely comforting. (Former US Defense Secretary, Casper Weinberger, 1982.)

The debate about 'star wars' has also touched the question of whether a technical solution to the nuclear arms race can be found that will replace the search for political solutions.

> There is no technological fix to the fraught and complex political relations between nations. There will never be an impermeable shield against nuclear evil. There is — and there has been for forty years — only one shield against chaos: that pitifully weak and yet somehow indestructable shield, the human conscience. It is as full of holes as a sieve, but it has kept chaos out for forty years. It is time to put it in repair. (Historian and anti-nuclear campaigner, E. P. Thompson, 1985.)

The idea of a system that would make nuclear attack impossible is very attractive, yet the technological challenge that such a programme presents is enormous. It is argued, however, that similar challenges have been met in the past; the development of the nuclear bomb for example. But, in an international system based on fear and distrust, can 'star wars' be confidently welcomed as a solution to the nuclear arms race?

8 Conclusion

Since 1945 we have lived with the existence of nuclear weapons, a military force powerful enough to destroy the world as we know it by killing most of the people on the planet, destroying both the environment and our old and rich civilizations. Over the past twenty years a number of additional problems have arisen which have encouraged many people to think more seriously about the prospect of a nuclear war actually occurring.

First, we have only recently emerged from one of the most dangerous periods since the Cold War first began in 1945 (see Introduction). For most of the 1980s hostile relations between the two superpowers, aggressive defence policies and intervention in other countries, such as Afghanistan, provided enormous obstacles in the search for a new *détente* such as existed in the early 1970s.

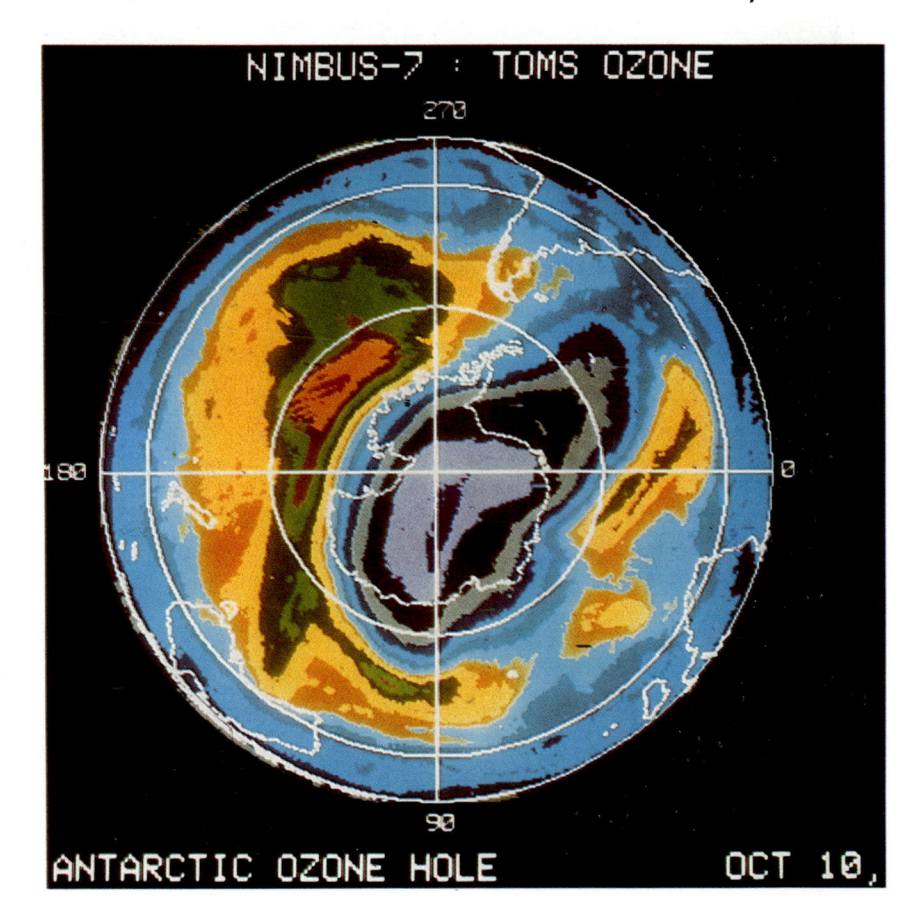

Left. *The hole in the ozone layer, (the purple area in the centre of the picture), as seen by a satellite. Environmental problems may cause additional political tensions between countries in the coming years.*

Above *Conflict between French security forces and anti-nuclear campaigners Greenpeace reached a peak in 1985. The Greenpeace flagship* Rainbow Warrior *is seen here sinking after being mined by the French secret service. They did this to ensure that the flagship did not interfere in nuclear tests that the French government was about to carry out.*

Second, there are the problems caused by countries developing or buying new weapons or defence systems. In the 1960s and 1970s there existed an uncomfortable, but relatively safe, 'mutual balance of terror', but if systems like SDI are allowed to develop, the balance might be destroyed. Furthermore, a number of military planners in the USA have recently talked about planning for and *winning* a nuclear war, rather than assuming that, once started, such a war would be catastrophic for both sides. This is despite evidence of the appalling casualties and long-lasting effects from the relatively small-scale nuclear strike against Japan in 1945 (see chapter two), and the evidence that a 'nuclear winter' could result from any but the smallest nuclear exchange. So, it is difficult to tell whether technical progress will help or hinder disarmament.

Third, there is the ever-present possibility that nuclear war or a serious nuclear incident could occur by accident. There are hundreds of examples of false alarms due mainly to technical errors (see information box page 13). During a period of increased political tension the threat of nuclear war by accident increases dramatically as more systems are placed on alert and as national leaders are faced with major, awkward decisions.

It is very clear that there are no easy answers when it comes to eliminating the threat of nuclear war. At present, hopes are based upon improved political relations between enemies and rivals — there is very little control over the numbers of weapons deployed. The essential problem lies in the fact that countries are still free to protect themselves in any way they please. There is no world government or set of binding laws that can stop either the spread or the use of nuclear weapons; the United Nations does not possess those powers. Nevertheless, during the late-1980s the United Nations has had more success in working towards peace, not just in relation to nuclear arms control, but also in the ending of the war in Afghanistan and the war between Iran and Iraq.

It is important not to think of nuclear war and nuclear weapons in isolation. Obviously, the most important threat of nuclear war comes from conflict between the Warsaw Pact and NATO. To a lesser extent wars in other parts of the world can also be a threat, if for example oil supplies are threatened, or close superpower allies such as Israel or Cuba are seen to be at risk. There is always the possibility that the outbreak of war in, for example, the Middle East would draw in the superpowers to such an extent that the conflict spills over into Europe, together with all the threats of nuclear war.

Life after nuclear war? 'Do you fancy another night in?'

Right *A peace march in Washington DC, USA, in support of a nuclear 'freeze'. Are such demands realistic, or will people simply have to get used to the idea of 'living with the bomb'?*

Below *President Eisenhower; he also warned us of the power of the arms industry.*

Equally, non-military problems could conceivably create the necessary conditions for nuclear war. Before the end of the century the world as a whole must face a range of vexing problems such as the pollution of the oceans; unpredictable changes in weather patterns caused by our thoughtless abuse of the environment; terrorism; the international debt crisis; the population crisis; recurring famines; and the overall problem of underdevelopment. The failure to solve these problems will increase levels of insecurity throughout the world and it is when nations and leaders begin to feel insecure that options such as war come to be seen as tempting solutions. In many ways all countries depend upon each other and the international system is full of direct and indirect connections. If this system begins to fall apart, as it so easily could, we will face an even greater threat from nuclear weapons. Perhaps in the end we will have to rely on the common sense of ordinary people around the world to coerce their governments into action.

> People in the long run are going to do more to promote peace than are governments. Indeed, I think that people want peace so much that one of these days governments had better get out of their way and let them have it. (Dwight D. Eisenhower, US President 1953-1961, September 1959.)

45

Glossary

Ally A country or person that is friendly, or countries that are joined together in a political or military alliance. Australia is an ally of New Zealand.

Anti-ballistic missile system A system designed to prevent nuclear weapons from hitting their targets. The 'star-wars' system is an anti-ballistic missile system.

Arsenal Stock of weapons.

Bilateral Something done by or affecting two people, things or countries. In this book bilateral usually refers to disarmament.

Civil defence The protection of civilians against the effects of disasters including nuclear war.

Component One small part of something.

Computer modelling Use of computers to try to predict what will happen in real life.

Conventional weapon Any weapon which is not nuclear.

Deploy To put military forces or equipment in place ready for use.

Détente The easing of strained relations between states.

Deterrence Preventing war or an attack on one's country by threatening a response to an aggressor. For example, threatening to use nuclear weapons to prevent another country from attacking.

Exigencies Urgent needs.

Fall-out Harmful radioactive dust that would settle after a nuclear explosion.

Hibakusha The Japanese word for the survivors of Hiroshima and Nagasaki.

Holocaust A large-scale destruction or massacre.

Impermeable Impossible to penetrate.

Impotent Useless, powerless.

INF Intermediate Nuclear Forces. Nuclear weapons with a range of 500 km–5500 km.

Megaton Measurement of a nuclear explosion; equal to one million tons of TNT explosive.

Mobilization Movements of troops and equipment immediately before a war.

Multilateral Something done by, or affecting, more than one country or alliance.

NATO The North Atlantic Treaty Organization. The military alliance that is made up of Belgium, Britain, Canada, Greece, Iceland, Italy, Luxembourg, the Netherlands, Norway, Portugal, Spain, Turkey, the USA and West Germany.

Non-Proliferation Treaty The treaty opened for signature in 1968 to prevent the spread of nuclear weapons.

Nullifying Making invalid or ineffective.

Obsolete Old; out of date; no longer used.

Partial Test Ban Treaty The agreement reached in 1963 by the superpowers and Britain not to carry out nuclear tests in the atmosphere, in space or underwater.

Plutonium Material for making nuclear weapons.

Pre-emptive strike The act of attacking first when it is feared that if you do not you will be attacked yourself.

Proliferate To multiply or increase in numbers. In this book *proliferation* refers to the increase in the numbers of nuclear weapons.

Prototype A trial model or early version of equipment.

Quaker A member of the Religious Society of Friends, a Christian Church which outlaws the use of violence.

Radiation sickness Internal damage to the body due to exposure to excessive doses of radioactive material, such as plutonium.

Strategic ballistic missile A nuclear weapon which is fired from one country, goes into space and returns to the earth's atmosphere before hitting its target.

Trillion One thousand billion (1,000,000,000,000).

Unilateral Something done by, or affecting, one person or group. (In this book unilateral usually refers to disarmament.)

Warsaw Pact The Warsaw Treaty Organization. The military alliance that is made up of Bulgaria, Czechoslovakia, East Germany, Hungary, Poland Romania and the Soviet Union.

Yield (In this context.) The size of a nuclear explosion.

Further information

You can contact these organizations to find out more about the issues covered in this book.

Armament and Disarmament Information Unit (ADIU), Mantell Building, University of Sussex, Falmer, Brighton, BN1 9RF, Britain

Arms Control and Disarmament Agency (ACDA), Washington DC, 20451, USA

Australian Peace Studies and Research Association (APSARA), 63 Mayfair Street, Mount Clairmont, WA, 6010, Australia

Canadian Centre for Arms Control and Disarmament, 151 Slater Street, Suite 710, Ottawa, Ontario, KP1 56H3, Canada

Further reading

For younger readers:

Briggs, R. *When the Wind Blows,* (Penguin, 1985)
Brown, A. *Nuclear Weapons,* (Wayland, 1987)
Campbell, C. *Nuclear Facts,* (Hamlyn, 1984)
Harbor, B. and Smith, C. *The Arms Trade,* (Wayland, 1988)
Heater, D. *The Cold War,* (Wayland, 1989)
Neild, R. *How To Make Up Your Mind About The Bomb,* (Deutsch, 1981)

For older readers:

Holroyd, F. (editor), *Thinking About Nuclear Weapons,* (Croom Helm, 1985)
Prins, G. *Defended to Death,* (Pelican, 1984)
Rogers, P. et al, *As Lambs to the Slaughter,* (Arrow, 1981)
Rumble, G. *The Politics of Nuclear Defence: A Comprehensive Introduction,* (Polity Press, 1985)
Sivard, R. *World Military and Social Expenditures 1987-1988,* (World Priorities, 1987)
Suddaby, A. *The Nuclear War Game,* (Longman, 1983)
Turner, J. *The Arms Race,* (Cambridge University Press, 1985)

Acknowledgements

The authors would like to thank Nina Williams for her helpful comments on an earlier draft of the manuscript.

The publishers gratefully acknowledge permission from the following to reproduce copyright material: the *Guardian* for an extract from an article by Richard Harris, Bishop of Oxford in the *Guardian,* 7 January, 1987; Housmans for an extract from *A Short Guide to Disarmament,* by Alan Litherman; *New Statesman and Society* for an extract from an article by Mary Kaldor in *New Statesman and Society,* 16 December, 1988; Pantheon Books for an extract from *The Game of Disarmament: How the United States and Russia Run the Nuclear Arms Race,* by Alva Myrdal; Sidgwick & Jackson for two extracts from *The Nuclear Winter* by Carl Sagan.

The publishers would like to thank the following for providing the illustrations in this book: Barnaby's Picture Library 14, 22, 30, 41 (top); BBC Hulton Picture Library 5; Camera Press 25, 45 (top); John Frost 26 (bottom); Geoscience Features 13; PHOTRI 11, 12 (top), 18, 19, 28 (top), 44; Popperfoto 4,6 (top), 10, 24 (bottom); The Research House 6 (bottom), 12 (bottom), 33, 35, 42; Rex Features 32 (bottom), 40, 43; Frank Spooner Pictures 37; Topham Picture Library *Cover,* 7, 8, 9, 17, 21, 23, 24 (top), 26 (top), 27, 29, 31, 32 (top), 34, 36 (bottom), 41 (bottom), 45 (bottom). The illustrations on pages 15, 16, 20 and 38 are by Marilyn Clay.

Index

Page numbers in **bold** refer to illustrations

Afghanistan 19, 42, 44
Anti-Ballistic Missile Treaty 40, 46
anti-nuclear protest 27, 28, 32, 35, 40, 45
Argentina 16
arms control 10, 30-37
arms race 18, 22, 29, 33, 36
atom bombs 4, 9-10, 16
Australia 6, 35

Biological Weapons Convention 31
Brazil 6, 16
Britain 5, 19, 25, 34

Campaign for Nuclear Disarmament (CND) 27
Canada 6, 35
chemical weapons **31**, 31
China 5, 6, 12, 19, 20, 25
civil defence 13-15, 46
Cold War 5, 42
conventional
    wars 19
    weapons 31
Cuba 6, 44
de Cuellar, Javier Pérez 25

disarmament 10, 25, 30-37
    bilateral 32
    multilateral 30, 32-3
    unilateral 29, 30, 47

Enola Gay **5**

France 5, 19, 25

Gorbachev, Mikhail **32**, **36**, 36-7, 40
Greenpeace **43**

Hiroshima 4, **8**, **9**, 9-10, **11**, 16, 18
India 6, 16, 19, 22, 25
Intermediate Nuclear Forces (INF) Treaty 32, 35, 46
Iran 16, 44
Iraq 16, 22, 44
Israel 20, 44

Japan 6, 9, 10, 12, 18, 43

Labour Party (British) **30**
Libya 16

Mount St Helens **13**

Nagasaki 4, **10**, 16
NATO 6, 7, 20, 31, 44, 46
    military exercise **17**
    nuclear policy 19
New Zealand 6, 7, 35
Non-Proliferation Treaty **24**, 24-5, 32
North Atlantic Treaty Organization see NATO
nuclear bombs 4, 9-10, 16
nuclear deterrence 14, 16-19, 28
nuclear shelters **14**, 14, **44**
nuclear tests **12**, **22**, 32, 47
nuclear war 43-5
    effects of 9-15
    fall-out 11, 46
    survivors **11**, 15
nuclear weapons
    accidents 13, 43
    arsenals 7, **16**, 29
    destruction of **33**, 37
    missiles
        Cruise 25
        Pershing II **33**
        Polaris 9

SS-12 **37**
    Trident **7**, **18**
    power of **15**
    proliferation 20, 20-25
    range **38**
    types 17
nuclear winter 12

Oppenheimer, Robert **4**, 4
ozone layer, hole in **42**

Pakistan 20, 22-3, 25
Partial Test Ban Treaty 32, 47

radiation 12, 13, 18, 46
Reagan, Ronald **32**, 38

SALT 32, 33-4
South Africa 16, 24
Soviet Union 5, 6, 47
    arms cuts 36-7
    international relations 19
    nuclear accidents 13
    nuclear weapons 5
'star wars' 23, 38-41, **39**
Strategic Arms Limitation Talks see SALT
Strategic Defence Initiative (SDI) see 'star wars'
Sweden 6
Switzerland 6

Thatcher, Margaret 17

United Nations 32, 44
USA 4, 5, 6, 12, 13, 19, 25, 40, 46
    nuclear policy 18-19, 43
    nuclear weapons 5, 16, 23
    'star wars' 38-41

Warsaw Pact 6, 7, 20, 36, 44, 46